The Civil War Poems

Walt Whitman

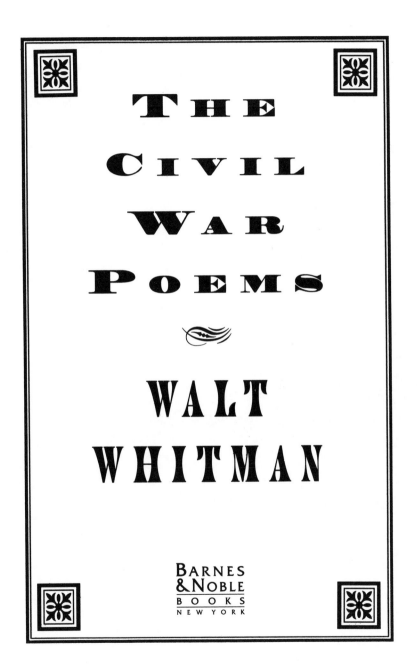

THE CIVIL WAR POEMS

WALT WHITMAN

BARNES
&NOBLE
BOOKS
NEW YORK

This edition published by Barnes & Noble, Inc.

1994 Barnes & Noble Books

Book design by James Sarfati

ISBN 1-56619-036-3

Printed and bound in the United States of America

M 9 8 7 6 5 4 3 2

✦ CONTENTS ✦

Memories of President Lincoln   1
   When Lilacs Last in the Dooryard Bloom'd   3
   O Captain! My Captain!   14
   Hush'd Be the Camps To-day   15
   This Dust Was Once the Man   16

Drum-Taps   17
   First O Songs for a Prelude   19
   Eighteen Sixty-One   22
   Beat! Beat! Drums!   23
   From Paumanok Starting I Fly Like a Bird   25
   Song of the Banner at Daybreak   26
   Rise, O Days, from Your Fathomless Deeps   34
   Virginia—the West   37
   City of Ships   38
   The Centenarian's Story   39
   Cavalry Crossing a Ford   45
   Bivouac on a Mountain Side   45
   An Army Corps on the March   46
   By the Bivouac's Fitful Flame   46
   Come up from the Fields Father   47
   Vigil Strange I Kept on the Field One Night   49
   A March in the Ranks Hard-Prest,
      and the Road Unknown   51

A Sight in Camp in the Daybreak Grey
  and Dim   53
As Toilsome I Wander'd Virginia's Woods   54
Not the Pilot   55
Year that Trembled and Reel'd beneath Me   55
The Wound-Dresser   56
Long, too Long, America   60
Give Me the Splendid Silent Sun   61
Dirge for Two Veterans   64
Over the Carnage Rose Prophetic a Voice   66
I Saw Old General at Bay   68
The Artilleryman's Vision   69
Ethiopia Saluting the Colours   71
Not Youth Pertains to Me   72
Race of Veterans   72
World Take Good Notice   73
O Tan-Faced Prairie-Boy   73
Look Down Fair Moon   74
Reconciliation   74
How Solemn As One by One   75
As I Lay with my Head in Your Lap,
  Camerado   76
Delicate Cluster   77
To a Certain Civilian   78
Lo, Victress on the Peaks   79
Spirit Whose Work is Done   80
Adieu to a Soldier   81
Turn O Libertad   82
To the Leaven'd Soil They Trod   83

Song of the Open Road   85

Index of First Lines   101

The Civil War Poems

Walt Whitman

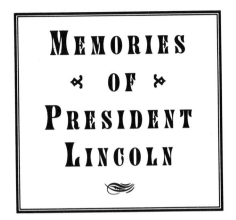

MEMORIES
❖ OF ❖
PRESIDENT
LINCOLN

When Lilacs Last in the Dooryard Bloom'd

1

When lilacs last in the dooryard bloom'd
And the great star early droop'd in the western sky in the night,
I mourn'd, and yet shall mourn with ever-returning spring.

Ever-returning spring, trinity sure to me you bring,
Lilac blooming perennial and drooping star in the west,
And thought of him I love.

2

O powerful western fallen star!
O shades of night—O moody, tearful night!
O great star disappear'd—O the black murk that hides the star!
O cruel hands that hold me powerless—O helpless soul of me!
O harsh surrounding cloud that will not free my soul.

3

In the dooryard fronting an old farm-house near the white-
    wash'd palings,
Stands the lilac-bush tall-growing with heart-shaped leaves of
    rich green,
With many a pointed blossom rising delicate, with the perfume
    strong I love,
With every leaf a miracle—and from this bush in the dooryard,
With delicate-colour'd blossoms and heart-shaped leaves of
    rich green,
A sprig with its flower I break.

4

In the swamp in secluded recesses,
A shy and hidden bird is warbling a song.
Solitary the thrush,
The hermit withdrawn to himself, avoiding the settlements,
Sings by himself a song.

Song of the bleeding throat,
Death's outlet song of life (for well, dear brother, I know,
If thou wast not granted to sing thou would'st surely die).

5

Over the breast of the spring, the land, amid cities,
Amid lanes and through old woods, where lately the violets
    peep'd from the ground, spotting the grey débris,
Amid the grass in the fields each side of the lanes, passing the
    endless grass,
Passing the yellow-spear'd wheat, every grain from its shroud in
    the dark-brown fields uprisen,
Passing the apple-tree blows of white and pink in the orchards,
Carrying a corpse to where it shall rest in the grave,
Night and day journeys a coffin.

6

Coffin that passes through lanes and streets,
Through day and night with the great cloud darkening the land,
With the pomp of the inloop'd flags with the cities draped in
    black,
With the show of the States themselves as of crape-veil'd women
    standing,
With processions long and winding and the flambeaus of the
    night,

With the countless torches lit, with the silent sea of faces and the
    unbared heads,
With the waiting depôt, the arriving coffin, and the sombre faces,
With dirges through the night, with the shout and voices rising
    strong and solemn,
With all the mournful voices of the dirges pour'd around the
    coffin,
The dim-lit churches and the shuddering organs—where amid
    these you journey,
With the tolling, tolling bells' perpetual clang,
Here, coffin that slowly passes,
I give you my sprig of lilac.

7

(Nor for you, for one alone,
Blossoms and branches green to coffins all I bring,
For fresh as the morning, thus would I chant a song for you,
    O sane and sacred death.

All over bouquets of roses,
O death, I cover you over with roses and early lilies,
But mostly and now the lilac that blooms the first,
Copious I break, I break the sprigs from the bushes,
With loaded arms I come, pouring for you,
For you and the coffins all of you, O death.)

8

O western orb, sailing the heaven,
Now I know what you must have meant as a month since
    I walk'd,
As I walk'd in silence the transparent shadowy night,

As I saw you had something to tell as you bent to me night after
    night,
As you droop'd from the sky low down as if to my side (while
    the other stars all look'd on),
As we wander'd together the solemn night (for something I know
    not what kept me from sleep),
As the night advanced, and I saw on the rim of the west how full
    you were of woe,
As I stood on the rising ground in the breeze in the cool
    transparent night,
As I watch'd where you pass'd and was lost in the netherward
    black of the night,
As my soul in its trouble dissatisfied sank, as where you, sad orb,
Concluded, dropt in the night, and was gone.

9

Sing on there in the swamp,
O singer, bashful and tender, I hear your notes, I hear your call,
I hear, I come presently, I understand you,
But a moment I linger, for the lustrous star has detain'd me,
The star my departing comrade holds and detains me.

10

O how shall I warble myself for the dead one there I loved?
And how shall I deck my song for the large sweet soul that has
    gone?
And what shall my perfume be for the grave of him I love?

Sea-winds blown from east and west,
Blown from the Eastern sea and blown from the Western sea, till
    there on the prairies meeting,

These and with these and the breath of my chant,
I'll perfume the grave of him I love.

11

O what shall I hang on the chamber walls?
And what shall the pictures be that I hang on the walls,
To adorn the burial-house of him I love?

Pictures of growing spring and farms and homes,
With the Fourth-month eve at sundown, and the grey smoke
    lucid and bright,
With floods of the yellow gold of the gorgeous, indolent, sinking
    sun, burning, expanding the air,
With the fresh sweet herbage under foot, and the pale green
    leaves of the trees prolific,
In the distance the flowing glaze, the breast of the river, with a
    wind-dapple here and there,
With ranging hills on the banks, with many a line against the
    sky, and shadows,
And the city at hand with dwellings so dense, and stacks of
    chimneys,
And all the scenes of life and the workshops, and the workmen
    homeward returning.

12

Lo, body and soul—this land,
My own Manhattan with spires, and the sparkling and hurrying
    tides, and the ships,
The varied and ample land, the South and the North in the light,
    Ohio's shores and flashing Missouri,
And ever the far-spreading prairies cover'd with grass and corn.

Lo, the most excellent sun so calm and haughty,
The violet and purple morn with just-felt breezes,
The gentle soft-born measureless light,
The miracle spreading bathing all, the fulfill'd noon,
The coming eve delicious, the welcome night and the stars,
Over my cities shining all, enveloping man and land.

13

Sing on, sing on, you grey-brown bird,
Sing from the swamps, the recesses, pour your chant from the
    bushes,
Limitless out of the dusk, out of the cedars and pines.

Sing on, dearest brother, warble your reedy song,
Loud human song, with voice of uttermost woe,

O liquid and free and tender!
O wild and loose to my soul—O wondrous singer!
You only I hear—yet the star holds me (but will soon depart),
Yet the lilac with mastering odour holds me.

14

Now while I sat in the day and look'd forth,
In the close of the day with its light and the fields of spring, and
    the farmers preparing their crops,
In the large unconscious scenery of my land with its lakes and
    forests,
In the heavenly aerial beauty (after the perturb'd winds and the
    storms),
Under the arching heavens of the afternoon swift passing, and
    the voices of children and women,
The many-moving sea-tides, and I saw the ships how they sail'd,

And the summer approaching with richness, and the fields all
    busy with labour,
And the infinite separate houses, how they all went on, each with
    its meals and minutia of daily usages,
And the streets how their throbbings throbb'd and the cities
    pent—lo, then and there,
Falling upon them all and among them all, enveloping me with
    the rest,
Appear'd the cloud, appear'd the long black trail,
And I knew death, its thought, and the sacred knowledge of
    death.

Then with the knowledge of death as walking one side of me,
And the thought of death close-walking the other side of me,
And I in the middle as with companions, and as holding the
    hands of companions,
I fled forth to the hiding receiving night that talks not,
Down to the shores of the water, the path by the swamp in the
    dimness,
To the solemn shadowy cedars and ghostly pines so still.

And the singer so shy to the rest receiv'd me,
The grey-brown bird I know receiv'd us comrades three,
And he sang the carol of death, and a verse for him I love.

From deep secluded recesses,
From the fragrant cedars and the ghostly pines so still,
Came the carol of the bird.

And the charm of the carol rapt me,
As I held as if by their hands my comrades in the night,
And the voice of my spirit tallied the song of the bird.

Come lovely and soothing death,
Undulate round the world, serenely arriving, arriving,
In the day, in the night, to all, to each,
Sooner or later delicate death.

Prais'd be the fathomless universe,
For life and joy, and for objects and knowledge curious,
And for love, sweet love—but praise! praise! praise!
For the sure-enwinding arms of cool-enfolding death.

Dark mother always gliding near with soft feet,
Have none chanted for thee a chant of fullest welcome?
Then I chant it for thee, I glorify thee above all,
I bring thee a song that when thou must indeed come, come unfalteringly.

Approach strong deliveress,
When it is so, when thou hast taken them I joyously sing the dead,
Lost in the loving floating ocean of thee,
Laved in the flood of thy bliss, O death.

From me to thee glad serenades,
Dances for thee I propose saluting thee, adornments and feastings
    for thee,
And the sights of the open landscape and the high-spread sky are fitting,
And life and the fields, and the huge and thoughtful night.

The night in silence under many a star,
The ocean shore and the husky whispering wave whose voice I know,
And the soul turning to thee, O vast and well-veil'd death,
And the body gratefully nestling close to thee.

Over the tree-tops I float thee a song,
Over the rising and sinking waves, over the myriad fields and the
    prairies wide,

Over the dense-pack'd cities all and the teeming wharves and ways,
I float this carol with joy, with joy to thee, O death.

15

To the tally of my soul,
Loud and strong kept up the grey-brown bird,
With pure deliberate notes spreading filling the night.

Loud in the pines and cedars dim,
Clear in the freshness moist and the swamp-perfume,
And I with my comrades there in the night.

While my sight that was bound in my eyes unclosed,
As to long panoramas of visions.

And I saw askant the armies,
I saw as in noiseless dreams hundreds of battle-flags,
Borne through the smoke of the battles and pierc'd with missiles
        I saw them,
And carried hither and yon through the smoke, and torn
        and bloody,
And at last but a few shreds left on the staffs (and all in silence),
And the staffs all splinter'd and broken.

I saw battle-corpses, myriads of them,
And the white skeletons of young men, I saw them,
I saw the débris and débris of all the slain soldiers of the war,
But I saw they were not as was thought,
They themselves were fully at rest, they suffer'd not,
The living remain'd and suffer'd, the mother suffer'd,
And the wife and the child and the musing comrade suffer'd,
And the armies that remain'd suffer'd.

16

Passing the visions, passing the night,
Passing, unloosing the hold of my comrades' hands,
Passing the song of the hermit bird and the tallying song of
    my soul,
Victorious song, death's outlet song, yet varying ever-altering
    song,
As low and wailing, yet clear the notes, rising and falling,
    flooding the night,
Sadly sinking and fainting, as warning and warning, and yet
    again bursting with joy,
Covering the earth and filling the spread of the heaven,
As that powerful psalm in the night I heard from recesses,
Passing, I leave thee lilac with heart-shaped leaves,
I leave thee there in the door-yard, blooming, returning
    with spring.

I cease from my song for thee,
From my gaze on thee in the west, fronting the west, communing
    with thee,
O comrade lustrous with silver face in the night.

Yet each to keep and all, retrievements out of the night,
The song, the wondrous chant of the grey-brown bird,
And the tallying chant, the echo arous'd in my soul,
With the lustrous and drooping star with the countenance full
    of woe,
With the holders holding my hand nearing the call of
    the bird,
Comrades mine and I in the midst, and their memory ever to
    keep, for the dead I loved so well,

For the sweetest, wisest soul of all my days and lands—and this
    for his dear sake,
Lilac and star and bird twined with the chant of my soul,
There in the fragrant pines and the cedars dusk and dim.

O Captain! My Captain!

O Captain! my Captain! our fearful trip is done,
The ship has weather'd every rack, the prize we sought is won,
The port is near, the bells I hear, the people all exulting,
While follow eyes the steady keel, the vessel grim and daring:
    But O heart! heart! heart!
      O the bleeding drops of red,
        Where on the deck my Captain lies,
        Fallen cold and dead.

O Captain! my Captain! rise up and hear the bells;
Rise up—for you the flag is flung—for you the bugle trills,
For you the bouquets and ribbon'd wreaths—for you the shores
    a-crowding,
For you they call, the swaying mass, their eager faces turning;
    Here Captain! dear father!
      This arm beneath your head!
        It is some dream that on the deck,
        You've fallen cold and dead.

My Captain does not answer, his lips are pale and still,
My father does not feel my arm, he has no pulse nor will,
The ship is anchor'd safe and sound, its voyage closed and done,
From fearful trip the victor ship comes in with object won;
    Exult, O shores, and ring, O bells!
      But I with mournful tread,
        Walk the deck my Captain lies,
        Fallen cold and dead.

Hush'd Be the Camps To-day

→ (*May 4, 1865*) ←

Hush'd be the camps to-day,
And soldiers, let us drape our war-worn weapons,
And each with musing soul retire to celebrate,
Our dear commander's death.

No more for him life's stormy conflicts,
Nor victory, nor defeat—no more time's dark events,
Charging like ceaseless clouds across the sky.

But sing, poet, in our name,
Sing of the love we bore him—because you, dweller in camps,
    know it truly.

As they invault the coffin there,
Sing—as they close the doors of earth upon him—one verse,
For the heavy hearts of soldiers.

This Dust Was Once the Man

This dust was once the man,
Gentle, plain, just, and resolute, under whose cautious hand,
Against the foulest crime in history known in any land or age,
Was saved the Union of these States.

DRUM-TAPS

First O Songs for a Prelude

First O songs for a prelude,
Lightly strike on the stretch'd tympanum pride and joy in
    my city,
How she led the rest to arms, how she gave the cue,
How at once with lithe limb unwaiting a moment she sprang,
(O superb! O Manhattan, my own, my peerless!
O strongest you in the hour of danger, in crisis! O truer
    than steel!)
How you sprang—how you threw off the costumes of peace with
    indifferent hand,
How your soft opera-music changed, and the drum and fife were
    heard in their stead,
How you led to the war (that shall serve for our prelude,
    songs of soldiers),
How Manhattan drum-taps led.

Forty years had I in my city seen soldiers parading,
Forty years as a pageant, till unawares the lady of this teeming
    and turbulent city,
Sleepless amid her ships, her houses, her incalculable wealth,
With her million children around her, suddenly,
At dead of night, at news from the south,
Incens'd struck with clinch'd hand the pavement.

A shock electric, the night sustain'd it,
Till with ominous hum our hive at daybreak pour'd out
    its myriads.

From the houses then and the workshops, and through all
    the doorways,
Leapt they tumultuous, and lo! Manhattan arming.

To the drum-taps prompt,

The young men falling in and arming,

The mechanics arming (the trowel, the jackplane, the black-
smith's hammer, tost aside with precipitation),

The lawyer leaving his office and arming, the judge leaving
the court,

The driver deserting his wagon in the street, jumping down,
throwing the reins abruptly down on the horses' backs,

The salesman leaving the store, the boss, bookkeeper, porter,
all leaving;

Squads gather everywhere by common consent and arm,

The new recruits, even boys, the old men show them how to
wear their accoutrements, they buckle the straps carefully,

Outdoors arming, indoors arming, the flash of the musket-barrels,

The white tents cluster in camps, the arm'd sentries around, the
sunrise cannon and again at sunset,

Arm'd regiments arrive every day, pass through the city, and
embark from the wharves,

(How good they look as they tramp down to the river, sweaty,
with their guns on their shoulders!

How I love them! how I could hug them, with their brown faces
and their clothes and knapsacks cover'd with dust!)

The blood of the city up—arm'd! arm'd! the cry everywhere,

The flags flung out from the steeples of churches and from all the
public buildings and stores,

The tearful parting, the mother kisses her son, the son kisses
his mother,

(Loth is the mother to part, yet not a word does she speak to
detain him),

The tumultuous escort, the ranks of policemen preceding, clearing
the way,

The unpent enthusiasm, the wild cheers of the crowd for
    their favourites,
The artillery, the silent cannons bright as gold, drawn along,
    rumble lightly over the stones,
(Silent cannons, soon to cease your silence,
Soon unlimber'd to begin the red business);
All the mutter of preparation, all the determin'd arming,
The hospital service, the lint, bandages, and medicines,
The women volunteering for nurses, the work begun for in
    earnest, no mere parade now;
War! an arm'd race is advancing! the welcome for battle, no
    turning away;
War! be it weeks, months, or years, an arm'd race is advancing
    to welcome it.

Mannahatta a-march—and it's O to sing it well!
It's O for a manly life in the camp.

And the sturdy artillery,
The guns bright as gold, the work for giants, to serve well
    the guns,
Unlimber them! (no more as the past forty years for salutes for
    courtesies merely,
Put in something now besides powder and wadding).
And you lady of ships, you Mannahatta,
Old matron of this proud, friendly, turbulent city,
Often in peace and wealth you were pensive or covertly frown'd
    amid all your children,
But now you smile with joy exulting old Mannahatta.

Eighteen Sixty-One

Arm'd year—year of the struggle,

No dainty rhymes or sentimental love verses for you, terrible
year,

Not you as some pale poetling seated at a desk lisping cadenzas
piano,

But as a strong man erect, clothed in blue clothes, advancing,
carrying a rifle on your shoulder,

With well-gristled body and sunburnt face and hands, with a
knife in the belt at your side,

As I heard you shouting loud, your sonorous voice ringing across
the continent,

Your masculine voice, O year, as rising amid the great cities,

Amid the men of Manhattan I saw you as one of the workmen,
the dwellers in Manhattan,

Or with large steps crossing the prairies out of Illinois and
Indiana,

Rapidly crossing the West with springy gait and descending the
Alleghanies,

Or down from the great lakes or in Pennsylvania, or on
deck along the Ohio river,

Or southward along the Tennessee or Cumberland rivers,
or at Chattanooga on the mountain top,

Saw I your gait and saw I your sinewy limbs clothed in blue,
bearing weapons, robust year,

Heard your determin'd voice launch'd forth again and again,

Year that suddenly sang by the mouths of the round-lipp'd
cannon,

I repeat you, hurrying, crashing, sad, distracted year.

Beat! Beat! Drums!

Beat! beat! drums!—blow! bugles! blow!
Through the windows—through doors—burst like a ruthless
    force,
Into the solemn church, and scatter the congregation,
Into the school where the scholar is studying;
Leave not the bridegroom quiet—no happiness must he have now
    with his bride,
Nor the peaceful farmer any peace, ploughing his field or
    gathering his grain,
So fierce you whirr and pound you drums—so shrill you bugles
    blow.

Beat! beat! drums!—blow! bugles! blow!
Over the traffic of cities—over the rumble of wheels in the
    streets;
Are beds prepared for sleepers at night in the houses? no
    sleepers must sleep in those beds,
No bargainers' bargains by day—no brokers or speculators—
    would they continue?
Would the talkers be talking? would the singer attempt to sing?
Would the lawyer rise in the court to state his case before the
    judge?
Then rattle quicker, heavier drums—you bugles wilder blow.

Beat! beat! drums!—blow! bugles! blow!
Make no parley—stop for no expostulation,
Mind not the timid—mind not the weeper or prayer,
Mind not the old man beseeching the young man,
Let not the child's voice be heard, nor the mother's entreaties,

Make even the trestles to shake the dead where they lie awaiting
the hearses,
So strong you thump, O terrible drums—so loud you bugles
blow.

From Paumanok Starting
I Fly Like a Bird

From Paumanok starting I fly like a bird,
Around and around to soar to sing the idea of all,
To the north betaking myself to sing there arctic songs,
To Kanada till I absorb Kanada in myself, to Michigan then,
To Wisconsin, Iowa, Minnesota, to sing their songs (they are
    inimitable);
Then to Ohio and Indiana to sing theirs, to Missouri and Kansas
    and Arkansas to sing theirs,
To Tennessee and Kentucky, to the Carolinas and Georgia to sing
    theirs,
To Texas and so along up toward California, to roam accepted
    everywhere;
To sing first (to the tap of the war-drum if need be),
The idea of all, of the Western world one and inseparable,
And then the song of each member of these States.

Song of the Banner at Daybreak

Poet

O a new song, a free song,
Flapping, flapping, flapping, flapping, by sounds, by voices
    clearer,
By the wind's voice and that of the drum,
By the banner's voice and child's voice and sea's voice and
    father's voice,
Low on the ground and high in the air,
On the ground where father and child stand,
In the upward air where their eyes turn,
Where the banner at daybreak is flapping.

Words! book-words! what are you?
Words no more, for hearken and see,
My song is there in the open air, and I must sing,
With the banner and pennant a-flapping.

I'll weave the chord and twine in,
Man's desire and babe's desire, I'll twine them in, I'll put in life,
I'll put the bayonet's flashing point, I'll let bullets and slugs
    whizz,
(As one carrying a symbol and menace far into the future,
Crying with trumpet voice, *Arouse and beware! Beware and arouse!*)
I'll pour the verse with streams of blood, full of volition, full
    of joy,
Then loosen, launch forth, to go and compete,
With the banner and pennant a-flapping.

Pennant

Come up here, bard, bard,
Come up here, soul, soul,

Come up here, dear little child,
To fly in the clouds and winds with me, and play with the
        measureless light.

Child

Father, what is that in the sky beckoning to me with long finger?
And what does it say to me all the while?

Father

Nothing, my babe, you see in the sky,
And nothing at all to you it says—but look you, my babe,
Look at these dazzling things in the houses, and see you the
        money-shops opening,
And see you the vehicles preparing to crawl along the streets
        with goods;
These, ah, these, how valued and toil'd for these!
How envied by all the earth.

Poet

Fresh and rosy red the sun is mounting high,
On floats the sea in distant blue careering through its channels,
On floats the wind over the breast of the sea setting in toward
        land,
The great steady wind from west or west-by-south,
Floating so buoyant with milk-white foam on the waters.

But I am not the sea nor the red sun,
I am not the wind with girlish laughter,
Not the immense wind which strengthens, not the wind which
        lashes,
Not the spirit that ever lashes its own body to terror and death,
But I am that which unseen comes and sings, sings, sings,

Which babbles in brooks and scoots in showers on the land,
Which the birds know in the woods mornings and evenings,
And the shore-sands know and the hissing wave, and that banner
   and pennant,
Aloft there flapping and flapping.

Child

O father it is alive—it is full of people—it has children,
O now it seems to me it is talking to its children,
I hear it—it talks to me—O it is wonderful!
O it stretches—it spreads and runs so fast—O my father,
It is so broad it covers the whole sky.

Father

Cease, cease, my foolish babe,
What you are saying is sorrowful to me, much it displeases me;
Behold with the rest again I say, behold not banners and pennants
   aloft,
But the well-prepared pavements behold, and mark the solid-wall'd
   houses.

Banner and Pennant

Speak to the child O bard out of Manhattan,
To our children all, or north or south of Manhattan,
Point this day, leaving all the rest, to us over all—and yet we
   know not why,
For what are we, mere strips of cloth profiting nothing,
Only flapping in the wind?

Poet

I hear and see not strips of cloth alone,
I hear the tramp of armies, I hear the challenging sentry,

I hear the jubilant shouts of millions of men, I hear Liberty!

I hear the drums beat and the trumpets blowing,

I myself move abroad swift-rising flying then,

I use the wings of the land-bird and use the wings of the sea-bird,
and look down as from a height,

I do not deny the precious results of peace, I see populous cities
with wealth incalculable,

I see numberless farms, I see the farmers working in their fields
or barns,

I see mechanics working, I see buildings everywhere founded,
going up, or finish'd,

I see trains of cars swiftly speeding along railroad tracks down by
the locomotives,

I see the stores, depôts, of Boston, Baltimore, Charleston,
New Orleans,

I see far in the West the immense area of grain, I dwell awhile
hovering,

I pass to the lumber forests of the North, and again to the
Southern plantation, and again to California;

Sweeping the whole I see the countless profit, the busy gatherings,
earn'd wages,

See the Identity formed out of thirty-eight spacious and haughty
States (and many more to come),

See forts on the shores of harbours, see ships sailing in and out;

Then over all (aye! aye!) my little and lengthen'd pennant shaped
like a sword,

Runs swiftly up indicating war and defiance—and now the
halyards have rais'd it,

Side of my banner broad and blue, side of my starry banner,

Discarding peace over all the sea and land.

Banner and Pennant

Yet louder, higher, stronger, bard! yet farther, wider cleave!
No longer let our children deem us riches and peace alone,
We may be terror and carnage, and are so now,
Not now are we any one of these spacious and haughty States (nor
  any five, nor ten),
Nor market nor depôt we, nor money-bank in the city,
But these and all, and the brown and spreading land, and the
  mines below, are ours,
And the shores of the sea are ours, and the rivers great and small,
And the fields they moisten, and the crops and the fruits are ours,
Bays and channels and ships sailing in and out are ours—while we
  over all,
Over the area spread below, the three or four millions of square
  miles, the capitals,
The forty millions of people,—O bard! in life and death supreme.
We, even we, henceforth flaunt out masterful, high up above,
Not for the present alone, for a thousand years chanting through
  you,
This song to the soul of one poor little child.

Child

O my father, I like not the houses,
They will never to me be anything, nor do I like money,
But to mount up there I would like, O father dear, that banner
  I like,
That pennant I would be and must be.

Father

Child of mine, you fill me with anguish,
To be that pennant would be too fearful,
Little you know what it is this day, and after this day, for ever,

It is to gain nothing, but risk and defy everything,
Forward to stand in front of wars—and O, such wars!—what have
   you to do with them?
With passions of demons, slaughter, premature death?

Banner

Demons and death then I sing,
Put in all, aye all will I, sword-shaped pennant for war,
And a pleasure new and ecstatic, and the prattled yearning of
   children,
Blent with the sounds of the peaceful land and the liquid wash of
   the sea,
And the black ships fighting on the sea envelop'd in smoke,
And the icy cool of the far, far north, with rustling cedars and
   pines,
And the whirr of drums and the sound of soldiers marching, and
   the hot sun shining south,
And the beach-waves combing over the beach on my Eastern
   shore, and my Western shore the same,
And all between those shores, and my ever running Mississippi
   with bends and chutes,
And my Illinois fields, and my Kansas fields, and my fields of
   Missouri,
The Continent, devoting the whole identity without reserving
   an atom,
Pour in! whelm that which asks, which sings, with all and the
   yield of all,
Fusing and holding, claiming, devouring the whole,
No more with tender lip, nor musical labial sound,
But out of the night emerging for good, our voice persuasive
   no more,
Croaking like crows here in the wind.

Poet

My limbs, my veins dilate, my theme is clear at last,
Banner so broad advancing out of the night, I sing you haughty
  and resolute,
I burst through where I waited long, too long, deafen'd
  and blinded,
My hearing and tongue are come to me (a little child taught me),
I hear from above, O pennant of war, your ironical call
  and demand,
Insensate! insensate! (yet I at any rate chant you) O banner!
Not houses of peace indeed are you, nor any nor all their
  prosperity (if need be, you shall again have every one of
  those houses to destroy them,
You thought not to destroy those valuable houses, standing fast,
  full of comfort, built with money,
May they stand fast, then? not an hour except you above them
  and all stand fast);
O banner, not money so precious are you, not farm produce you,
  nor the material good nutriment,
Nor excellent stores, nor landed on wharves from the ships,
Not the superb ships with sail-power or steam-power, fetching and
  carrying cargoes,
Nor machinery, vehicles, trade, nor revenues—but you as
  henceforth I see you,
Running up out of the night, bringing your cluster of stars
  (ever-enlarging stars),
Divider of daybreak you, cutting the air, touch'd by the sun,
  measuring the sky,
(Passionately seen and yearn'd for by one poor little child,
While other remain busy or smartly talking, for ever teaching
  thrift, thrift);

O you up there! O pennant! where you undulate like a snake
hissing so curious,
Out of reach, an idea only, yet furiously fought for, risking bloody
death, loved by me,
So loved—O you banner leading the day with stars brought from
the night!
Valueless, object of eyes, over all and demanding all—(absolute
owner of all)—O banner and pennant!
I too leave the rest—great as it is, it is nothing—houses, machines
are nothing—I see them not,
I see but you, O warlike pennant! O banner so broad, with
stripes, I sing you only,
Flapping up there in the wind.

Rise, O Days, from Your Fathomless Deeps

1

Rise, O days, from your fathomless deeps, till you loftier, fiercer
    sweep,

Long for my soul hungering gymnastic I devour'd what the earth
    gave me,

Long I roam'd the woods of the north, long I watch'd Niagara
    pouring,

I travell'd the prairies over and slept on their breast, I cross'd the
    Nevadas, I cross'd the plateaus,

I ascended the towering rocks along the Pacific, I sail'd out to
    sea,

I sail'd through the storm, I was refresh'd by the storm,

I watch'd with joy the threatening maws of the waves,

I mark'd the white combs where they career'd so high, curling
    over,

I heard the wind piping, I saw the black clouds,

Saw from below what arose and mounted (O superb! O wild as
    my heart, and powerful!),

Heard the continuous thunder as it bellow'd after the lightning,

Noted the slender and jagged threads of lightning as sudden and
    fast amid the din they chased each other across the sky;

These, and such as these, I, elate, saw—saw with wonder, yet
    pensive and masterful,

All the menacing might of the globe uprisen around me,

Yet there with my soul I fed, I fed content, supercilious.

2

'Twas well, O soul—'twas a good preparation you gave me,
Now we advance our latent and ampler hunger to fill,
Now we go forth to receive what the earth and the sea never
gave us,
Not through the mighty woods we go, but through the mightier
cities,
Something for us is pouring now more than Niagara pouring,
Torrents of men (sources and rills of the North-west, are you
indeed inexhaustible?),
What, to pavements and homesteads here, what were those
storms of the mountains and sea?
What, to passions I witness around me to-day? was the sea
risen?
Was the wind piping the pipe of death under the black clouds?
Lo! from deeps more unfathomable, something more deadly and
savage,
Manhattan rising, advancing with menacing front—Cincinnati,
Chicago, unchain'd;
What was that swell I saw on the ocean? behold what comes
here,
How it climbs with daring feet and hands—how it dashes!
How the true thunder bellows after the lightning—how bright the
flashes of lightning!
How Democracy with desperate vengeful port strides on, shown
through the dark by those flashes of lightning!
(Yet a mournful wail and low sob I fancied I heard through the
dark,
In a lull of the deafening confusion.)

3

Thunder on! stride on, Democracy! strike with vengeful stroke!
And do you rise higher than ever yet, O days, O cities!
Crash heavier, heavier yet, O storms! you have done me good,
My soul prepared in the mountains absorbs your immortal strong nutriment,
Long had I walk'd my cities, my country roads through farms, only half satisfied,
One doubt nauseous undulating like a snake, crawl'd on the ground before me,
Continually preceding my steps, turning upon me oft, ironically hissing low;
The cities I loved so well I abandon'd and left, I sped to the certainties suitable to me,
Hungering, hungering, hungering, for primal energies and Nature's dauntlessness,
I refresh'd myself with it only, I could relish it only,
I waited the bursting forth of the pent fire—on the water and air I waited long;
But now I no longer wait, I am fully satisfied, I am glutted,
I have witness'd the true lightning, I have witness'd my cities electric,
I have lived to behold man burst forth and warlike America rise,
Hence I will seek no more the food of the northern solitary wilds,
No more the mountains roam or sail the stormy sea.

Virginia—the West

The noble sire fallen on evil days,
I saw with hand uplifted, menacing, brandishing,
(Memories of old in abeyance, love and faith in abeyance),
The insane knife toward the Mother of All.

The noble son on sinewy feet advancing,
I saw, out of the land of prairies, land of Ohio's waters and
        of Indiana,
To the rescue the stalwart giant hurry his plenteous offspring,
Drest in blue, bearing their trusty rifles on their shoulders.

Then the Mother of All with calm voice speaking,
As to you Rebellious (I seemed to hear her say), why strive
        against me, and why seek my life?
When you yourself for ever provide to defend me?
For you provided me Washington—and now these also.

City of Ships

City of ships!
(O the black ships! O the fierce ships!
O the beautiful sharp-bow'd steamships and sail-ships!)
City of the world! (for all races are here,
All the lands of the earth make contributions here);
City of the sea! city of hurried and glittering tides!
City whose gleeful tides continually rush or recede, whirling in
    and out with eddies and foam!
City of wharves and stores—city of tall façades of marble and
    iron!
Proud and passionate city—mettlesome, mad,extravagant city!
Spring up, O city—not for peace alone, but be indeed yourself,
    warlike!
Fear not—submit to no models but your own, O city!
Behold me—incarnate me as I have incarnated you!
I have rejected nothing you offer'd me—whom you adopted I
    have adopted,
Good or bad I never question you—I love all—I do not condemn
    anything,
I chant and celebrate all that is yours—yet peace no more,
In peace I chanted peace, but now the drum of war is mine,
War, red war is my song through your streets, O city!

The Centenarian's Story

Volunteer of 1861-2 (at Washington Park, Brooklyn, assisting the Centenarian)

Give me your hand, old Revolutionary,
The hill-top is nigh, but a few steps (make room, gentlemen),
Up the path you have follow'd me well, spite of your hundred
and extra years,
You can walk, old man, though your eyes are almost done,
Your faculties serve you, and presently I must have them
serve me.

Rest, while I tell what the crowd around us means,
On the plain below recruits are drilling and exercising,
There is the camp, one regiment departs tomorrow,
Do you hear the officers giving their orders?
Do you hear the clank of the muskets?

Why, what comes over you now, old man?
Why do you tremble and clutch my hand so convulsively?
The troops are but drilling, they are yet surrounded with smiles,
Around them at hand the well-drest friends and the women,
While splendid and warm the afternoon sun shines down,
Green the midsummer verdure and fresh blows the dallying
breeze,
O'er proud and peaceful cities and arm of the sea between.

But drill and parade are over, they march back to quarters,
Only hear that approval of hands! hear what a clapping!

As wending the crowds now part and disperse — but we, old man,
Not for nothing have I brought you hither — we must remain,
You to speak in your turn, and I to listen and tell.

The Centenarian

When I clutch'd your hand it was not with terror,
But suddenly pouring about me here on every side,
And below there where the boys were drilling, and up the slopes
    they ran,
And where tents are pitch'd, and wherever you see south and
    south-east and south-west,
Over hill, across lowlands, and in the skirts of woods,
And along the shores, in mire (now fill'd over) came again and
    suddenly raged,
As eighty-five years a-gone no mere parade receiv'd with applause
    of friends,
But a battle which I took part in myself—aye, long ago as it is, I
    took part in it,
Walking then this hill-top, this same ground.

Aye, this is the ground,
My blind eyes even as I speak behold it re-peopled from graves,
The years recede, pavements and stately houses disappear,
Rude forts appear again, the old hoop'd guns are mounted,
I see the lines of rais'd earth stretching from river to bay,
I mark the vista of waters, I mark the uplands and slopes;
Here we lay encamp'd, it was this time in summer also.

As I talk I remember all, I remember the Declaration,
It was read here, the whole army paraded, it was read to us here,
By his staff surrounded the General stood in the middle, he held
    up his unsheath'd sword,
It glitter'd in the sun in full sight of the army.

'Twas a bold act then—the English war-ships had just arrived,
We could watch down the lower bay where they lay at anchor,
And the transports swarming with soldiers.

A few days more and they landed, and then the battle.

Twenty thousand were brought against us,
A veteran force furnish'd with good artillery.

I tell not now the whole of the battle,
But one brigade early in the forenoon order'd forward to engage
    the red-coats,
Of that brigade I tell, and how steadily it march'd,
And how long and well it stood confronting death.

Who do you think that was marching steadily sternly confronting
    death?
It was the brigade of the youngest men, two thousand strong,
Rais'd in Virginia and Maryland, and most of them known
    personally to the General.

Jauntily forward they went with quick step toward Gowanus'
    waters,
Till of a sudden unlook'd for by defiles through the woods, gain'd
    at night,
The British advancing, rounding in from the east, fiercely playing
    their guns,
That brigade of the youngest was cut off and at the enemy's
    mercy.

The General watch'd them from this hill,
They made repeated desperate attempts to burst their environment,
Then drew close together, very compact, their flag flying in the
    middle,
But O from the hills how the cannon were thinning and thinning
    them!

It sickens me yet, that slaughter!
I saw the moisture gather in drops on the face of the General,
I saw how he wrung his hands in anguish.

Meanwhile the British manoeuvr'd to draw us out for a
pitch'd battle,
But we dared not trust the chances of a pitch'd battle.

We fought the fight in detachments,
Sallying forth we fought at several points, but in each the luck was
against us,
Our foe advancing, steadily getting the best of it, push'd us back
to the works on this hill,
Till we turn'd menacing here, and then he left us.

That was the going out of the brigade of the youngest men, two
thousand strong,
Few return'd, nearly all remain in Brooklyn.

That and here my General's first battle,
No women looking on nor sunshine to bask in, it did not conclude
with applause,
Nobody clapp'd hands here then.

But in darkness, in mist on the ground under a chill rain,
Wearied that night we lay foil'd and sullen,
While scornfully laugh'd many an arrogant lord off against us
encamp'd,
Quite within hearing, feasting, clinking wine-glasses together over
their victory.

So dull and damp and another day,
But the night of that, mist lifting, rain ceasing,
Silent as a ghost while they thought they were sure of him, my
General retreated.

I saw him at the river-side,
Down by the ferry lit by torches, hastening the embarcation;

My General waited till the soldiers and wounded were all
    pass'd over,
And then (it was just ere sunrise), these eyes rested on him for the
    last time.

Every one else seemed fill'd with gloom,
Many no doubt thought of capitulation.

But when my General pass'd me,
As he stood in his boat and look'd toward the coming sun,
I saw something different from capitulation.

Terminus

Enough, the Centenarian's story ends,
The two, the past and present, have interchanged,
I myself as connecter, as chansonnier of a great future, am
    now speaking.

And is this the ground Washington trod?
And these waters I listlessly daily cross, are these the waters
    he cross'd,
As resolute in defeat as other generals in their proudest triumphs?

I must copy the story, and send it eastward and westward,
I must preserve that look as it beam'd on you rivers of Brooklyn.

See — as the annual round returns the phantoms return,
It is the 27th of August and the British have landed,
The battle begins and goes against us, behold through the smoke
    Washington's face,
The brigade of Virginia and Maryland have march'd forth to
    intercept the enemy,
They are cut off, murderous artillery from the hills plays
    upon them,

Rank after rank falls, while over them silently droops the flag,
Baptized that day in many a young man's bloody wounds,
In death, defeat, and sisters', mothers' tears.

Ah, hills and slopes of Brooklyn! I perceive you are more valuable
    than your owners supposed;
In the midst of you stands an encampment very old,
Stands for ever the camp of that dead brigade.

Cavalry Crossing a Ford

A line in long array where they wind betwixt green islands,
They take a serpentine course, their arms flash in the sun—hark
 to the musical clank,
Behold the silvery river, in it the splashing horses loitering stop
 to drink,
Behold the brown-faced men, each group, each person a picture,
 the negligent rest on the saddles,
Some emerge on the opposite bank, others are just entering the
 ford—while,
Scarlet and blue and snowy white,
The guidon flags flutter gaily in the wind.

Bivouac on a Mountain Side

I see before me now a travelling army halting,
Below a fertile valley spread, with barns and the orchards
 of summer,
Behind, the terraced sides of a mountain, abrupt, in places
 rising high,
Broken, with rocks, with clinging cedars, with tall shapes
 dingily seen,
The numerous camp-fires scatter'd near and far, some away up
 on the mountain,
The shadowy forms of men and horses, looming, large-sized,
 flickering,
And over all the sky—the sky! far, far out of reach, studded,
 breaking out, the eternal stars.

An Army Corps on the March

With its cloud of skirmishers in advance,
With now the sound of a single shot snapping like a whip, and
    now an irregular volley,
The swarming ranks press on and on, the dense brigades
    press on,
Glittering dimly, toiling under the sun—the dust-cover'd men,
In columns rise and fall to the undulations of the ground,
With artillery interspers'd—the wheels rumble, the horses sweat,
As the army corps advances.

By the Bivouac's Fitful Flame

By the bivouac's fitful flame,
A procession winding around me, solemn and sweet and slow—
    but first I note,
The tents of the sleeping army, the fields' and woods'
    dim outline,
The darkness lit by spots of kindled fire, the silence,
Like a phantom far or near an occasional figure moving,
The shrubs and trees (as I lift my eyes they seem to be stealthily
    watching me),
While wind in procession thoughts, O tender and wondrous
    thoughts,
Of life and death, of home and the past and loved, and of those
    that are far away;
A solemn and slow procession there as I sit on the ground,
By the bivouac's fitful flame.

Come up from the Fields Father

Come up from the fields father, here's a letter from our Pete,
And come to the front door, mother, here's a letter from thy
  dear son.

Lo, 'tis autumn,
Lo, where the trees, deeper green, yellower and redder,
Cool and sweeten Ohio's villages with leaves fluttering in the
  moderate wind,
Where apples ripe in the orchards hang and grapes on the
  trellis'd vines,
(Smell you the smell of the grapes on the vines?
Smell you the buckwheat where the bees were lately buzzing?)

Above all, lo, the sky so calm, so transparent after the rain, and
  with wondrous clouds,
Below too, all calm, all vital and beautiful, and the farm prospers
  well.

Down in the fields all prospers well,
But now from the fields come, father, come at the daughter's call,
And come to the entry, mother, to the front door come right
  away.

Fast as she can she hurries, something ominous, her steps
  trembling,
She does not tarry to smooth her hair nor adjust her cap.

Open the envelope quickly,
O this is not our son's writing, yet his name is sign'd,
O a strange hand writes for our dear son, O stricken mother's
  soul!
All swims before her eyes, flashes with black, she catches the
  main words only,

Sentences broken, *gunshot wound in the breast, cavalry skirmish,
     taken to hospital,*
At present low, but will soon be better.

Ah, now the single figure to me,
Amid all teeming and wealthy Ohio with all its cities and farms,
Sickly white in the face and dull in the head, very faint,
By the jamb of a door leans.

Grieve not so, dear mother (the just-grown daughter speaks through
     her sobs,
The little sisters huddle around speechless and dismay'd),
See, dearest mother, the letter says Pete will soon be better.

Alas, poor boy, he will never be better (nor maybe needs to be
     better, that brave and simple soul),
While they stand at home at the door he is dead already,
The only son is dead.

But the mother needs to be better,
She with thin form presently drest in black,
By day her meals untouch'd, then at night fitfully sleeping, often
     waking,
In the midnight waking, weeping, longing with one deep longing,
O that she might withdraw unnoticed, silent from life escape and
     withdraw,
To follow, to seek, to be with her dear dead son.

Vigil Strange I Kept
on the Field One Night

Vigil strange I kept on the field one night;

When you, my son and my comrade, dropt at my side that day,

One look I but gave which your dear eyes return'd with a look I
    shall never forget,

One touch of your hand to mine, O boy, reach'd up as you lay
    on the ground,

Then onward I sped in the battle, the even-contested battle,

Till late in the night reliev'd to the place at last again I made
    my way,

Found you in death so cold, dear comrade, found your body, son
    of responding kisses (never again on earth responding),

Bared your face in the starlight, curious the scene, cool blew the
    moderate night-wind,

Long there and then in vigil I stood, dimly around me the
    battle-field spreading,

Vigil wondrous and vigil sweet there in the fragrant silent night,

But not a tear fell, not even a long-drawn sigh, long, long
    I gazed,

Then on the earth partially reclining sat by your side leaning my
    chin in my hands,

Passing sweet hours, immortal and mystic hours with you,
    dearest comrade—not a tear, not a word,

Vigil of silence, love and death, vigil for you, my son and my
    soldier,

As onward silently stars aloft, eastward new ones upward stole,

Vigil final for you, brave boy (I could not save you, swift was
    your death,

I faithfully loved you and cared for you living, I think we shall
    surely meet again),
Till at latest lingering of the night, indeed just as the dawn
    appear'd,
My comrade I wrapt in his blanket, envelop'd well his form,
Folded the blanket well, tucking it carefully over head and
    carefully under feet,
And there and then and bathed by the rising sun, my son in his
    grave, in his rude-dug grave I deposited,
Ending my vigil strange with that, vigil of night and battlefield
    dim,
Vigil for boy of responding kisses (never again on earth
    responding),
Vigil for comrade swiftly slain, vigil I never forget, how as day
    brighten'd,
I rose from the chill ground and folded my soldier well in his
    blanket,
And buried him where he fell.

A March in the Ranks Hard-Prest, and the Road Unknown

A march in the ranks hard-prest, and the road unknown,
A route through a heavy wood, with muffled steps in the
darkness,
Our army foil'd with loss severe, and the sullen remnant
retreating,
Till after midnight glimmer upon us the lights of a dim-lighted
building,
We come to an open space in the woods, and halt by the dim-
lighted building,
'Tis a large old church at the crossing roads, now an impromptu
hospital,
Entering but for a minute I see a sight beyond all the pictures
and poems ever made,
Shadows of deepest, deepest black, just lit by moving candles and
lamps,
And by one great pitchy torch stationary with wild red flame and
clouds of smoke,
By these, crowds, groups of forms vaguely I see on the floor,
some in the pews laid down,
At my feet more distinctly a soldier, a mere lad, in danger of
bleeding to death (he is shot in the abdomen),
I stanch the blood temporarily (the youngster's face is white
as a lily),
Then before I depart I sweep my eyes o'er the scene fain to
absorb it all,
Faces, varieties, postures beyond description, most in obscurity,
some of them dead,

Surgeons operating, attendants holding lights, the smell of ether, the odour of blood,
The crowd, O the crowd of the bloody forms, the yard outside also fill'd,
Some on the bare ground, some on planks or stretchers, some in the death-spasm sweating,
An occasional scream or cry, the doctor's shouted orders or calls,
The glisten of the little steel instruments catching the glint of the torches,
These I resume as I chant, I see again the forms, I smell the odour,
Then hear outside the orders given, *Fall in, my men, fall in;*
But first I bend to the dying lad, his eyes open, a half-smile gives he me,
Then the eyes close, calmly close, and I speed forth to the darkness,
Resuming, marching, ever in darkness marching, on in the ranks,
The unknown road still marching.

A Sight in Camp
in the Daybreak Grey and Dim

A sight in camp in the daybreak grey and dim,
As from my tent I emerge so early sleepless,
As slow I walk in the cool fresh air the path near by the hospital
    tent,
Three forms I see on stretchers lying, brought out there untended
    lying,
Over each the blanket spread, ample brownish woollen blanket,
Grey and heavy blanket, folding, covering all.

Curious I halt and silent stand,
Then with light fingers I from the face of the nearest the first just
    lift the blanket;
Who are you elderly man so gaunt and grim, with well-grey'd
    hair, and flesh all sunken about the eyes?
Who are you, my dear comrade?

Then to the second I step—and who are you, my child and
    darling?
Who are you sweet boy with cheeks yet blooming?

Then to the third—a face nor child nor old, very calm, as of
    beautiful yellow-white ivory;
Young man, I think I know you—I think this face is the face of
    the Christ himself,
Dead and divine and brother of all, and here again he lies.

As Toilsome I Wander'd Virginia's Woods

As toilsome I wander'd Virginia's woods,
To the music of rustling leaves kick'd by my feet (for 'twas
    autumn),
I mark'd at the foot of a tree the grave of a soldier;
Mortally wounded he and buried on the retreat (easily all could
    I understand),
The halt of a mid-day hour, when up! no time to lose—yet this
    sign left,
On a tablet scrawl'd and nail'd on the tree by the grave,
Bold, cautious, true, and my loving comrade.

Long, long I muse, then on my way go wandering,
Many a changeful season to follow, and many a scene of life,
Yet at times through changeful season and scene, abrupt, alone,
    or in the crowded street,
Comes before me the unknown soldier's grave, comes the
    inscription rude in Virginia's woods,
Bold, cautious, true, and my loving comrade.

Not the Pilot

Not the pilot has charged himself to bring his ship into port,
     though beaten back and many times baffled;
Not the pathfinder penetrating inland weary and long,
By deserts parch'd, snows chill'd, rivers wet, perseveres till he
     reaches his destination,
More than I have charged myself, heeded or unheeded, to
     compose a march for these States,
For a battle-call, rousing to arms if need be, years,
     centuries hence.

Year that Trembled and Reel'd beneath Me

Year that trembled and reel'd beneath me!
Your summer wind was warm enough, yet the air I breathed
     froze me,
A thick gloom fell through the sunshine and darken'd me,
Must I change my triumphant songs? said I to myself,
Must I indeed learn to chant the cold dirges of the baffled?
And sullen hymns of defeat?

The Wound-Dresser

1

An old man bending I come among new faces,
Years looking backward resuming in answer to children,
Come tell us, old man, as from young men and maidens that
    love me,
(Arous'd and angry, I'd thought to beat the alarum, and urge
    relentless war,
But soon my fingers fail'd me, my face droop'd and I resign'd
    myself,
To sit by the wounded and soothe them, or silently watch the
    dead;)
Years hence of these scenes, of these furious passions, these
    chances,
Of unsurpass'd heroes (was one side so brave? the other was
    equally brave;)
Now be witness again, paint the mightiest armies of earth,
Of those armies so rapid, so wondrous, what saw you to tell us?
What stays with you latest and deepest? of curious panics,
Of hard-fought engagements or sieges tremendous what deepest
    remains?

2

O maidens and young men I love and that love me,
What you ask of my days those the strangest and sudden your
    talking recalls,
Soldier alert I arrive after a long march cover'd with sweat and
    dust,
In the nick of time I come, plunge in the fight, loudly shout in
    the rush of successful charge,

Enter the captur'd works—yet lo, like a swift-running river
     they fade,
Pass and are gone they fade—I dwell not on soldiers' perils or
     soldiers' joys,
(Both I remember well—many the hardships, few the joys, yet I
     was content).

But in silence, in dreams' projections,
While the world of gain and appearance and mirth goes on,
So soon what is over forgotten, and waves wash the imprints off
     the sand,
With hinged knees returning I enter the doors (while for you
     up there,
Whoever you are, follow without noise and be of strong heart).

Bearing the bandages, water and sponge,
Straight and swift to my wounded I go,
Where they lie on the ground after the battle brought in,
Where their priceless blood reddens the grass, the ground,
Or to the rows of the hospital tent, or under the roof'd hospital,
To the long rows of cots up and down each side I return,
To each and all one after another I draw near, not one do I miss,
An attendant follows holding a tray, he carries a refuse pail,
Soon to be fill'd with clotted rags and blood, emptied, and
     fill'd again.

I onward go, I stop,
With hinged knees and steady hand to dress wounds,
I am firm with each, the pangs are sharp yet unavoidable,
One turns to me his appealing eyes—poor boy!
I never knew you,
Yet I think I could not refuse this moment to die for you, if that
     would save you.

3

On, on I go (open doors of time! open hospital doors!)
The crush'd head I dress (poor crazed hand tear not the bandage
    away),
The neck of the cavalry-man with the bullet through and through
    I examine,
Hard the breathing rattles, quite glazed already the eye, yet life
    struggles hard,
(Come sweet death! be persuaded O beautiful death!
In mercy come quickly).

From the stump of the arm, the amputated hand,
I undo the clotted lint, remove the slough, wash off the matter
    and blood,
Back on his pillow the soldier bends with curv'd neck and side-
    falling head,
His eyes are closed, his face is pale, he dares not look on the
    bloody stump,
And has not yet look'd on it.

I dress a wound in the side, deep, deep,
But a day or two more, for see the frame all wasted and sinking,
And the yellow-blue countenance see.

I dress the perforated shoulder, the foot with the bullet-wound,
Cleanse the one with a gnawing and putrid gangrene, so
    sickening, so offensive,
While the attendant stands behind aside me holding the tray and
    pail.

I am faithful, I do not give out,
The fractur'd thigh, the knee, the wound in the abdomen,

These and more I dress with impassive hand (yet deep in my
    breast a fire, a burning flame).

4

Thus in silence in dreams' projections,
Returning, resuming, I thread my way through the hospitals,
The hurt and wounded I pacify with soothing hand,
I sit by the restless all the dark night, some are so young,
Some suffer so much, I recall the experience sweet and sad,
(Many a soldier's loving arms about this neck have cross'd and
    rested,
Many a soldier's kiss dwells on these bearded lips).

Long, too Long, America

Long, too long, America,

Travelling roads all even and peaceful you learn'd from joys and
prosperity only,

But now, ah now, to learn from crises of anguish, advancing,
grappling with direst fate and recoiling not,

And now to conceive and show to the world what your children
en-masse really are,

(For who except myself has yet conceiv'd what your children
en-masse really are?)

Give Me the Splendid Silent Sun

Give me the splendid silent sun with all his beams full-dazzling,
Give me juicy autumnal fruit ripe and red from the orchard,
Give me a field where the unmow'd grass grows,
Give me an arbour, give me the trellis'd grape,
Give me fresh corn and wheat, give me serene-moving animals
    teaching content,
Give me nights perfectly quiet as on high plateaus west of the
    Mississippi, and I looking up at the stars,
Give me odorous at sunrise a garden of beautiful flowers where I
    can walk undisturb'd,
Give me for marriage a sweet-breath'd woman of whom I should
    never tire,
Give me a perfect child, give me away aside from the noise of the
    world a rural domestic life,
Give me to warble spontaneous songs recluse by myself, for my
    own ears only,
Give me solitude, give me Nature, give me again O Nature your
    primal sanities!

These demanding to have them (tired with ceaseless excitement,
    and rack'd by the war-strife),
These to procure incessantly asking, rising in cries from my
    heart,
While yet incessantly asking still I adhere to my city,
Day upon day and year upon year, O city, walking your streets,
Where you hold me enchain'd a certain time refusing to give
    me up,
Yet giving to make me glutted, enrich'd of soul, you give me
    forever faces;

(O I see what I sought to escape, confronting, reversing my cries,
I see my own soul trampling down what it ask'd for).

2

Keep your splendid silent sun,
Keep your woods, O Nature, and the quiet places by the woods,
Keep your fields of clover and timothy, and your corn-fields and
    orchards,
Keep the blossoming buckwheat fields where the Ninth-month
    bees hum;
Give me faces and streets—give me these phantoms incessant and
    endless along the trottoirs!
Give me interminable eyes—give me women—give me comrades
    and lovers by the thousand!
Let me see new ones every day—let me hold new ones by the
    hand every day!
Give me such shows—give me the streets of Manhattan!
Give me Broadway, with the soldiers marching—give me the
    sound of the trumpets and drums!
(The soldiers in companies or regiments—some starting away,
    rush'd and reckless,
Some, their time up, returning with thinn'd ranks, young, yet
    very old, worn, marching, noticing nothing;)
Give me the shores and wharves heavy-fringed with black ships!
O such for me! O an intense life, full to repletion and varied!
The life of the theatre, bar-room, huge hotel, for me!
The saloon of the steamer! the crowded excursion for me! the
    torchlight procession!
The dense brigade bound for the war, with high piled military
    wagons following;
People, endless, streaming, with strong voices, passions, pageants,

Manhattan streets with their powerful throbs, with beating drums
as now,
The endless and noisy chorus, the rustle and clank of muskets
(even the sight of the wounded),
Manhattan crowds, with their turbulent musical chorus!
Manhattan faces and eyes forever for me.

Dirge for Two Veterans

The last sunbeam
Lightly falls from the finish'd Sabbath,
On the pavement here, and there beyond it is looking,
    Down a new-made double grave.

    Lo, the moon ascending,
Up from the east the silvery round moon,
Beautiful over the house-tops, ghastly, phantom moon,
    Immense and silent moon.

    I see a sad procession,
And I hear the sound of coming full-key'd bugles,
All the channels of the city streets they're flooding,
    As with voices and with tears.

    I hear the great drums pounding,
And the small drums steady whirring,
And every blow of the great convulsive drums,
    Strikes me through and through.

    For the son is brought with the father,
(In the foremost ranks of the fierce assault they fell,
Two veterans son and father dropt together,
    And the double grave awaits them).

    Now nearer blow the bugles,
And the drums strike more convulsive,
And the daylight o'er the pavement quite has faded,
    And the strong dead-march enwraps me.

    In the eastern sky up-buoying,
The sorrowful vast phantom moves illumin'd,

('Tis some mother's large transparent face,
  In heaven brighter glowing).

O strong dead-march, you please me!
O moon immense with your silvery face, you soothe me!
O my soldiers twain! O my veterans passing to burial!
What I have I also give you.

The moon gives you light,
And the bugles and the drums give you music,
And my heart, O my soldiers, my veterans,
  My heart gives you love.

Over the Carnage
Rose Prophetic a Voice

Over the carnage rose prophetic a voice,
Be not dishearten'd, affection shall solve the problems of
    freedom yet,
Those who love each other shall become invincible,
They shall yet make Columbia victorious.

Sons of the Mother of All, you shall yet be victorious,
You shall yet laugh to scorn the attacks of all the remainder of
    the earth.

No danger shall balk Columbia's lovers,
If need be a thousand shall sternly immolate themselves for one.

One from Massachusetts shall be a Missourian's comrade,
From Maine and from hot Carolina, and another an Oregonese,
    shall be friends triune,
More precious to each other than all the riches of the earth.

To Michigan, Florida perfumes shall tenderly come,
Not the perfumes of flowers, but sweeter, and wafted
    beyond death.

It shall be customary in the houses and streets to see manly
    affection,
The most dauntless and rude shall touch face to face lightly,
The dependence of Liberty shall be lovers,
The continuance of Equality shall be comrades.

These shall tie you and band you stronger than hoops of iron,
I, ecstatic, O partners! O lands! with the love of lovers tie you.

(Were you looking to be held together by lawyers?
Or by an agreement on a paper? or by arms?
Nay, nor the world, nor any living thing, will so cohere.)

I Saw Old General at Bay

I saw old General at bay,
(Old as he was, his grey eyes yet shone out in battle like stars),
His small force was not completely hemmed in, in his works,
He call'd for volunteers to run the enemy's lines, a desperate
    emergency,
I saw a hundred and more step forth from the ranks, but two or
    three were selected,
I saw them receive their orders aside, they listen'd with care, the
    adjutant was very grave,
I saw them depart with cheerfulness, freely risking their lives.

The Artilleryman's Vision

While my wife at my side lies slumbering, and the wars are
over long,
And my head on the pillow rests at home, and the vacant
midnight passes,
And through the stillness, through the dark, I hear, just hear, the
breath of my infant,
There in the room as I wake from sleep this vision presses
upon me;
The engagement opens there and then in fantasy unreal,
The skirmishers begin, they crawl cautiously ahead, I hear the
irregular snap! snap!
I hear the sound of the different missiles, the short *t-h-t! t-h-t!* of
the rifle-balls,
I see the shells exploding leaving small white clouds, I hear the
great shells shrieking as they pass,
The grape like the hum and whirr of wind through the trees
(tumultuous now the contest rages),
All the scenes at the batteries rise in detail before me again,
The crashing and smoking, the pride of the men in their pieces,
The chief-gunner ranges and sights his piece and selects a fuse of
the right time,
After firing I see him lean aside and look eagerly off to note the
effect;
Elsewhere I hear the cry of a regiment charging (the young
colonel leads himself this time with brandish'd sword),
I see the gaps cut by the enemy's volleys (quickly fill'd up, no
delay),
I breathe the suffocating smoke, then the flat clouds hover low
concealing all;

Now a strange lull for a few seconds, not a shot fired on
     either side,
Then resumed the chaos louder than ever, with eager calls and
     orders of officers,
While from some distant part of the field the wind wafts to my
     ears a shout of applause (some special success),
And ever the sound of the cannon far or near (rousing even in
     dreams a devilish exultation and all the old mad joy in the
     depths of my soul),
And ever the hastening of infantry shifting positions, batteries,
     cavalry, moving hither and thither,
(The falling, dying, I heed not, the wounded dripping and red I
     heed not, some to the rear are hobbling),
Grime, heat, rush, aide-de-camps galloping by or on a full run,
With the patter of small arms, the warning *s-s-t* of the rifles
     (these in my vision I hear or see),
And bombs bursting in air, and at night the vari-colour'd rockets.

Ethiopia Saluting the Colours

Who are you, dusky woman, so ancient hardly human,
With your woolly-white and turban'd head, and bare bony feet?
Why rising by the roadside here, do you the colours greet?

('Tis while our army lines Carolina's sands and pines,
Forth from thy hovel door thou, Ethiopia, com'st to me,
As under doughty Sherman I march toward the sea.)

Me master years a hundred since from my parents sunder'd,
A little child, they caught me as the savage beast is caught,
Then hither me across the sea the cruel slaver brought.

No further does she say, but lingering all the day,
Her high-borne turban'd head she wags, and rolls her
      darkling eye,
And courtesies to the regiments, the guidons moving by.

What is it, fateful woman, so blear, hardly human?
Why wag your head with turban bound, yellow, red, and green?
Are the things so strange and marvellous you see or have seen?

Not Youth Pertains to Me

Not youth pertains to me,
Nor delicatesse, I cannot beguile the time with talk,
Awkward in the parlour, neither a dancer nor elegant,
In the learn'd coterie sitting constrain'd and still, for learning
    inures not to me,
Beauty, knowledge, inure not to me—yet there are two or three
    things inure to me,
I have nourish'd the wounded and sooth'd many a dying soldier
And at intervals waiting or in the midst of camp,
Composed these songs.

Race of Veterans

Race of veterans—race of victors!
Race of the soil, ready for conflict—race of the conquering
    march!
(No more credulity's race, abiding-temper'd race),
Race henceforth owning no law but the law of itself,
Race of passion and the storm.

World Take Good Notice

World take good notice, silver stars fading,
Milky hue ript, weft of white detaching,
Coals thirty-eight, baleful and burning,
Scarlet, significant, hands off warning,
Now and henceforth flaunt from these shores.

O Tan-Faced Prairie-Boy

O tan-faced prairie-boy,
Before you came to camp came many a welcome gift,
Praises and presents came and nourishing food, till at last among
  the recruits,
You came, taciturn, with nothing to give—we but look'd on each
  other,
When lo! more than all the gifts of the world you gave me.

Look Down Fair Moon

Look down fair moon, and bathe this scene,
Pour softly down night's nimbus floods on faces ghastly,
    swollen, purple,
On the dead on their backs with arms toss'd wide,
Pour down your unstinted nimbus, sacred moon.

Reconciliation

Word over all, beautiful as the sky,
Beautiful that war and all its deeds of carnage must in time be
    utterly lost,
That the hands of the sisters Death and Night incessantly softly
    wash again, and ever again, this soil'd world;
For my enemy is dead, a man divine as myself is dead,
I look where he lies white-faced and still in the coffin—I draw
    near,
Bend down and touch lightly with my lips the white face in
    the coffin.

How Solemn As One by One

→ (*Washington City*, 1865) ←

How solemn as one by one,
As the ranks returning worn and sweaty, as the men file by
where I stand,
As the faces the masks appear, as I glance at the faces studying
the masks
(As I glance upward out of this page studying you, dear friend,
whoever you are),
How solemn the thought of my whispering soul to each in the
ranks, and to you,
I see behind each mask that wonder a kindred soul,
O the bullet could never kill what you really are, dear friend,
Nor the bayonet stab what you really are;
The soul! yourself I see, great as any, good as the best,
Waiting secure and content, which the bullet could never kill,
Nor the bayonet stab, O friend.

As I Lay with my Head in Your Lap, Camerado

As I lay with my head in your lap, camerado,

The confession I made I resume, what I said to you and the open
air I resume,

I know I am restless and make others so,

I know my words are weapons full of danger, full of death,

For I confront peace, security, and all the settled laws, to unsettle
them,

I am more resolute because all have denied me than I could ever
have been had all accepted me,

I heed not and have never heeded either experience, cautions,
majorities, nor ridicule,

And the threat of what is call'd hell is little or nothing to me,

And the lure of what is call'd heaven is little or nothing to me;

Dear camerado! I confess I have urged you onward with me, and
still urge you, without the least idea what is our destination,

Or whether we shall be victorious, or utterly quell'd and
defeated.

Delicate Cluster

Delicate cluster! flag of teeming life!
Covering all my lands—all my seashores lining!
Flag of death! (how I watch'd you through the smoke of battle
    pressing!
How I heard you flap and rustle, cloth defiant!)
Flag cerulean—sunny flag, with the orbs of night dappled!
Ah, my silvery beauty—ah, my woolly white and crimson!
Ah, to sing the song of you, my matron mighty!
My sacred one, my mother.

To a Certain Civilian

Did you ask dulcet rhymes from me?
Did you seek the civilian's peaceful and languishing rhymes?
Did you find what I sang erewhile so hard to follow?
Why I was not singing erewhile for you to follow, to
    understand—nor am I now;
(I have been born of the same as the war was born,
The drum-corps' rattle is ever to me sweet music, I love well the
    martial dirge,
With slow wail and convulsive throb leading the officer's
    funeral;)
What to such as you anyhow such a poet as I? therefore leave
    my works,
And go lull yourself with what you can understand, and with
    piano-tunes,
For I lull nobody, and you will never understand me.

Lo, Victress on the Peaks

Lo, Victress on the peaks,
Where thou with mighty brow regarding the world,
(The world, O Libertad, that vainly conspired against thee),
Out of its countless beleaguering toils, after thwarting them all,
Dominant, with the dazzling sun around thee,
Flauntest now unharm'd in immortal soundness and bloom—lo, in
　　these hours supreme,
No poem proud, I chanting bring to thee, nor mastery's
　　rapturous verse,
But a cluster containing night's darkness and blood-dripping
　　wounds,
And psalms of the dead.

Spirit Whose Work is Done

→ (*Washington City*, 1865) ←

Spirit whose work is done—spirit of dreadful hours!
Ere departing fade from my eyes your forests of bayonets;
Spirit of gloomiest fears and doubts (yet onward ever unfaltering
    pressing),
Spirit of many a solemn day and many a savage scene—electric
    spirit,
That with muttering voice through the war now closed, like a
    tireless phantom flitted,
Rousing the land with breath of flame, while you beat and beat
    the drum,
Now as the sound of the drum, hollow and harsh to the last,
    reverberates round me,
As your ranks, your immortal ranks, return, return from the
    battles,
As the muskets of the young men yet lean over their shoulders,
As I look on the bayonets bristling over their shoulders,
As those slanted bayonets, whole forests of them appearing in the
    distance, approach and pass on, returning homeward,
Moving with steady motion, swaying to and fro to the right
    and left,
Evenly lightly rising and falling while the steps keep time;
Spirit of hours I knew, all hectic red one day, but pale as death
    next day,
Touch my mouth ere you depart, press my lips close,
Leave me your pulses of rage—bequeath them to me—fill me
    with currents convulsive,
Let them scorch and blister out of my chants when you are gone,
Let them identify you to the future in these songs.

Adieu to a Soldier

Adieu, O soldier,
You of the rude campaigning (which we shared),
The rapid march, the life of the camp,
The hot contention of opposing fronts, the long manoeuvre,
Red battles with their slaughter, the stimulus, the strong terrific
    game,
Spell of all brave and manly hearts, the trains of time through
    you and like of you all fill'd,
With war and war's expression.

Adieu, dear comrade,
Your mission is fulfill'd—but I, more warlike,
Myself and this contentious soul of mine,
Still on our own campaigning bound.
Through untried roads with ambushes, opponents lined,
Through many a sharp defeat and many a crisis, often baffled,
Here marching, ever marching on, a war fight out—aye here,
To fiercer, weightier battles give expression.

Turn O Libertad

Turn O Libertad, for the war is over,

From it and all henceforth expanding, doubting no more,
    resolute, sweeping the world,

Turn from lands retrospective recording proofs of the past,

From the singers that sing the trailing glories of the past,

From the chants of the feudal world, the triumphs of kings,
    slavery, caste,

Turn to the world, the triumphs reserv'd and to come—give up
    that backward world,

Leave to the singers of hitherto, give them the trailing past,

But what remains remains for singers for you—wars to come are
    for you,

(Lo, how the wars of the past have duly inured to you, and the
    wars of the present also inure;)

Then turn, and be not alarm'd, O Libertad—turn your
    undying face,

To where the future, greater than all the past,

Is swiftly, surely preparing for you.

To the Leaven'd Soil They Trod

To the leaven'd soil they trod calling I sing for the last

(Forth from my tent emerging for good, loosing, untying the tent-
ropes),

In the freshness the forenoon air, in the far-stretching circuits
and vistas again to peace restored,

To the fiery fields emanative and the endless vistas beyond, to the
South and the North,

To the leaven'd soil of the general Western world to attest my
songs,

To the Alleghanian hills and the tireless Mississippi,

To the rocks I calling sing, and all the trees in the woods,

To the plains of the poems of heroes, to the prairies spreading
wide,

To the far-off sea and the unseen winds, and the sane impalpable
air;

And responding they answer all (but not in words),

The average earth, the witness of war and peace, acknowledges
mutely,

The prairie draws me close, as the father to bosom broad the son,

The Northern ice and rain that began me nourish me to the end,

But the hot sun of the South is to fully ripen my songs.

SONG
✤ OF ✤
THE OPEN
ROAD

Song of the Open Road

1

Afoot and light-hearted I take to the open road,
Healthy, free, the world before me,
The long brown path before me leading wherever I choose.

Henceforth I ask not good-fortune, I myself am good-fortune,
Henceforth I whimper no more, postpone no more, need nothing,
Done with indoor complaints, libraries, querulous criticisms,
Strong and content I travel the open road.

The earth, that is sufficient,
I do not want the constellations any nearer,
I know they are very well where they are,
I know they suffice for those who belong to them.

(Still here I carry my old delicious burdens,
I carry them, men and women, I carry them with me wherever
    I go,
I swear it is impossible for me to get rid of them,
I am fill'd with them, and I will fill them in return.)

2

You road I enter upon and look around, I believe you are not all
    that is here,
I believe that much unseen is also here.

Here the profound lesson of reception, nor preference nor denial,
The black with his woolly head, the felon, the diseas'd, the
    illiterate person, are not denied;
The birth, the hasting after the physician, the beggar's tramp, the
    drunkard's stagger, the laughing party of mechanics,

The escaped youth, the rich person's carriage, the fop, the
    eloping couple,
The early market-man, the hearse, the moving of furniture into
    the town, the return back from the town,
They pass, I also pass, anything passes, none can be interdicted,
None but are accepted, none but shall be dear to me.

3

You air that serves me with breath to speak!
You objects that call from diffusion my meanings and give them
    shape!
You light that wraps me and all things in delicate equable
    showers!
You paths worn in the irregular hollows by the roadsides!
I believe you are latent with unseen existences, you are so dear
    to me.

You flagg'd walks of the cities! you strong curbs at the edges!
You ferries! you planks and posts of wharves! you timber-lined
    sides! you distant ships!
You rows of houses! you window-pierc'd façades! you roofs!
You porches and entrances! you copings and iron guards!
You windows whose transparent shells might expose so much!
You doors and ascending steps! you arches!
You grey stones of interminable pavements! you trodden
    crossings!
From all that has touch'd you I believe you have imparted to
    yourselves, and now would impart the same secretly to me,
From the living and the dead you have peopled your impassive
    surfaces, and the spirits thereof would be evident and
    amicable with me.

4

The earth expanding right hand and left hand,
The picture alive, every part in its best light,
The music falling in where it is wanted, and stopping where it is
    not wanted,
The cheerful voice of the public road, the gay fresh sentiment of
    the road.

O highway I travel, do you say to me, *Do not leave me?*
Do you say, *Venture not—if you leave me you are lost?*
Do you say, *I am already prepared, I am well-beaten and undenied,*
    adhere to me?

O public road, I say back I am not afraid to leave you, yet
    I love you,
You express me better than I can express myself,
You shall be more to me than my poem.

I think heroic deeds were all conceiv'd in the open air, and all
    free poems also,
I think I could stop here myself and do miracles,
I think whatever I shall meet on the road I shall like, and
    whoever beholds me shall like me.
I think whoever I see must be happy.

5

From this hour I ordain myself loos'd of limits and imaginary
    lines,
Going where I list, my own master total and absolute,
Listening to others, considering well what they say,
Pausing, searching, receiving, contemplating,

Gently, but with undeniable will, divesting myself of the holds
    that would hold me.

I inhale great draughts of space,
The east and the west are mine, and the north and the south
    are mine.

I am larger, better than I thought,
I did not know I held so much goodness.

All seems beautiful to me,
I can repeat over to men and women, You have done such good
    to me I would do the same to you,
I will recruit for myself and you as I go,
I will scatter myself among men and women as I go,
I will toss a new gladness and roughness among them,
Whoever denies me it shall not trouble me,
Whoever accepts me he or she shall be blessed and shall
    bless me.

6

Now if a thousand perfect men were to appear it would not
    amaze me,
Now if a thousand beautiful forms of women appear'd it would
    not astonish me.

Now I see the secret of the making of the best persons,
It is to grow in the open air and to eat and sleep with the earth.

Here a great personal deed has room,
(Such a deed seizes upon the hearts of the whole race of men,
Its effusion of strength and will overwhelms law and mocks all
    authority and all argument against it).

Here is the test of wisdom,
Wisdom is not finally tested in schools,

Wisdom cannot be pass'd from one having it to another not
   having it,
Wisdom is of the soul, is not susceptible of proof, is its own
   proof,
Applies to all stages and objects and qualities and is content,
Is the certainty of the reality and immortality of things, and the
   excellence of things;
Something there is in the float of the sight of things that
   provokes it out of the soul.

Now I re-examine philosophies and religions,
They may prove well in lecture-rooms, yet not prove at all under
   the spacious clouds and along the landscape and flowing
   currents.

Here is realisation,
Here is a man tallied—he realises here what he has in him,
The past, the future, majesty, love—if they are vacant of you,
   you are vacant of them.

Only the kernel of every object nourishes;
Where is he who tears off the husks for you and me?
Where is he that undoes stratagems and envelopes for you
   and me?

Here is adhesiveness, it is not previously fashion'd, it is apropos;
Do you know what it is as you pass to be loved by strangers?
Do you know the talk of those turning eyeballs?

7

Here is the efflux of the soul,
The efflux of the soul comes from within through embower'd
   gates, ever provoking questions,
These yearnings why are they? these thoughts in the darkness
   why are they?

Why are there men and women that while they are nigh me the
    sunlight expands my blood?
Why when they leave me do my pennants of joy sink flat and
    lank?
Why are there trees I never walk under but large and melodious
    thoughts descend upon me?
(I think they hang there winter and summer on those trees and
    always drop fruit as I pass);
What is it I interchange so suddenly with strangers?
What with some driver as I ride on the seat by his side?
What with some fisherman drawing his seine by the shore as I
    walk by and pause?
What give me to be free to a woman's and man's good-will? what
    gives them to be free to mine?

8

The efflux of the soul is happiness, here is happiness,
I think it pervades the open air, waiting at all times,
Now it flows unto us, we are rightly charged.

Here rises the fluid and attaching character,
The fluid and attaching character is the freshness and sweetness
    of man and woman,
(The herbs of the morning sprout no fresher and sweeter every
    day out of the roots of themselves, than it sprouts fresh and
    sweet continually out of itself).
Toward the fluid and attaching character exudes the sweat of the
    love of young and old,
From it falls distill'd the charm that mocks beauty and
    attainments,
Toward it heaves the shuddering, longing ache of contact.

9

Allons! whoever you are come travel with me!
Travelling with me you find what never tires.

The earth never tires,
The earth is rude, silent, incomprehensible at first, Nature is rude
and incomprehensible at first,
Be not discouraged, keep on, there are divine things well
envelop'd,
I swear to you there are divine things more beautiful than words
can tell.

Allons! we must not stop here,
However sweet these laid-up stores, however convenient this
dwelling we cannot remain here,
However shelter'd this port and however calm these waters we
must not anchor here,
However welcome the hospitality that surrounds us we are
permitted to receive it but a little while.

10

Allons! the inducements shall be greater,
We will sail pathless and wild seas,
We will go where winds blow, waves dash, and the Yankee
clipper speeds by under full sail.

Allons! with power, liberty, the earth, the elements,
Health, defiance, gaiety, self-esteem, curiosity;
Allons! from all formules!
From your formules, O bat-eyed and materialistic priests.

The stale cadaver blocks up the passage—the burial waits
no longer.

Allons! yet take warning!
He travelling with me needs the best blood, thews, endurance,
None may come to the trial till he or she bring courage and
    health,
Come not here if you have already spent the best of yourself,
Only those may come who come in sweet and determin'd bodies,
No diseas'd person, no rum-drinker or venereal taint is permitted
    here.

(I and mine do not convince by arguments, similes, rhymes,
We convince by our presence.)

11

Listen! I will be honest with you,
I do not offer the old smooth prizes, but offer rough new prizes,
These are the days that must happen to you:
You shall not heap up what is call'd riches,
You shall scatter with lavish hand all that you earn or achieve,
You but arrive at the city to which you were destin'd, you hardly
    settle yourself to satisfaction before you are call'd by an
    irresistible call to depart,
You shall be treated to the ironical smiles and mockings of those
    who remain behind you,
What beckonings of love you receive you shall only answer with
    passionate kisses of parting,
You shall not allow the hold of those who spread their reach'd
    hands toward you.

12

Allons! after the great Companions, and to belong to them!
They too are on the road—they are the swift and majestic men—
    they are the greatest women,

Enjoyers of calms of seas and storms of seas,
Sailors of many a ship, walkers of many a mile of land,
Habitués of many distant countries, habitués of far-distant
dwellings,
Trusters of men and women, observers of cities, solitary toilers,
Pausers and contemplators of tufts, blossoms, shells of the shore,
Dancers at wedding-dances, kissers of brides, tender helpers of
children, bearers of children,
Soldiers of revolts, standers by gaping graves, lowerers-down of
coffins,
Journeyers over consecutive seasons, over the years, the curious
years each emerging from that which preceded it,
Journeyers as with companions, namely their own diverse phases,
Forth-steppers from the latent unrealised baby-days,
Journeyers gaily with their own youth, journeyers with their
bearded and well-grain'd manhood,
Journeyers with their womanhood, ample, unsurpass'd, content,
Journeyers with their own sublime old age of manhood or
womanhood,
Old age, calm, expanded, broad with the haughty breadth of the
universe,
Old age, flowing free with the delicious nearby freedom of death.

13

Allons! to that which is endless as it was beginningless,
To undergo much, tramps of days, rests of nights,
To merge all in the travel they tend to, and the days and nights
they tend to,
Again to merge them in the start of superior journeys,
To see nothing anywhere but what you may reach it and pass it,
To conceive no time, however distant, but what you may reach it
and pass it,

To look up or down no road but it stretches and waits for you,
however long but it stretches and waits for you,
To see no being, not God's or any, but you also go thither,
To see no possession but you may possess it, enjoying all without
labour or purchase, abstracting the feast yet not abstracting
one particle of it,
To take the best of the farmer's farm and the rich man's elegant
villa, and the chaste blessings of the well-married couple,
and the fruits of orchards and flowers of gardens,
To take to your use out of the compact cities as you pass
through,
To carry buildings and streets with you afterward wherever
you go,
To gather the minds of men out of their brains as you encounter
them, to gather the love out of their hearts,
To take your lovers on the road with you, for all that you leave
them behind you,
To know the universe itself as a road, as many roads, as roads
for travelling souls.

All parts away for the progress of souls,
All religion, all solid things, arts, governments—all that was or is
apparent upon this globe or any globe, falls into niches and
corners before the procession of souls along the grand roads
of the universe.

Of the progress of the souls of men and women along the grand
roads of the universe, all other progress is the needed
emblem and sustenance.

Forever alive, forever forward,
Stately, solemn, sad, withdrawn, baffled, mad, turbulent, feeble,
dissatisfied,

Desperate, proud, fond, sick, accepted by men, rejected by
men,
They go! they go! I know that they go, but I know not where
they go,
But I know that they go toward the best—toward something
great.

Whoever you are, come forth! or man or woman come forth!
You must not stay sleeping and dallying there in the house,
though you built it, or though it has been built for you.

Out of the dark confinement! out from behind the screen!
It is useless to protest, I know all and expose it.

Behold through you as bad as the rest,
Through the laughter, dancing, dining, supping of people,
Inside of dresses and ornaments, inside of those wash'd and
trimm'd faces,
Behold a secret silent loathing and despair.

No husband, no wife, no friend, trusted to hear the confession,
Another self, a duplicate of every one, skulking and hiding it
goes,
Formless and wordless through the streets of the cities, polite and
bland in the parlours,
In the cars of railroads, in steamboats, in the public assembly,
Home to the houses of men and women, at the table, in the
bedroom, everywhere,
Smartly attired, countenance smiling, form upright, death under
the breast-bones, hell under the skull-bones,
Under the broadcloth and gloves, under the ribbons and artificial
flowers,

Keeping fair with the customs, speaking not a syllable of itself,
Speaking of anything else but never of itself.

14

Allons! through struggles and wars!
The goal that was named cannot be countermanded.

Have the past struggles succeeded?
What has succeeded? yourself? your nation? Nature?
Now understand me well—it is provided in the essence of things
    that from any fruition of success, no matter what, shall
    come forth something to make a greater struggle necessary.

My call is the call of battle, I nourish active rebellion,
He going with me must go well arm'd,
He going with me goes often with spare diet, poverty, angry
    enemies, desertions.

15

Allons! the road is before us!
It is safe—I have tried it—my own feet have tried it well—be not
    detain'd!
Let the paper remain on the desk unwritten, and the book on the
    shelf unopen'd!

Let the tools remain in the workshop! let the money remain
    unearn'd!
Let the school stand! mind not the cry of the teacher!

Let the preacher preach in his pulpit! let the lawyer plead in the
    court, and the judge expound the law.

Camerado, I give you my hand!
I give you my love more precious than money,
I give you myself before preaching or law;
Will you give me yourself? will you come travel with me?
Shall we stick by each other as long as we live?

✣ INDEX OF FIRST LINES ✦

A line in long array where they wind betwixt green
   islands   45

A march in the ranks hard-prest, and the road
   unknown   51

A sight in camp in the daybreak grey and dim   53

Adieu, O soldier   81

Afoot and light-hearted I take to the open road   87

An old man bending I come among new faces   56

Arm'd year—year of the struggle   22

As I lay with my head in your lap, camerado   76

As toilsome I wander'd Virginia's woods   54

Beat! beat! drums!—blow! bugles! blow!   23

By the bivouac's fitful flame   46

City of ships!   38

Come up from the fields father, here's a letter from
   our Pete   47

Delicate cluster! flag of teeming life!   77

Did you ask dulcet rhymes from me?   78

First O songs for a prelude   19

From Paumanok starting I fly like a bird   25

Give me the splendid silent sun with all his beams
  full-dazzling   61

Give me your hand, old Revolutionary   39

How solemn as one by one   75

Hush'd be the camps to-day   15

I saw old General at bay   68

I see before me now a travelling army halting   45

Lo, Victress on the peaks   79

Long, too long, America   60

Look down fair moon, and bathe this scene   74

Not the pilot has charged himself to bring his ship
  into port, though beaten back and many times
  baffled   55

Not youth pertains to me   72

O a new song, a free song   26

O Captain! my Captain! our fearful trip is done   14

O tan-faced prairie-boy   73

Over the carnage rose prophetic a voice   66

Race of veterans—race of victors!   72

Rise, O days, from your fathomless deeps, till you
  loftier, fiercer sweep   34

Spirit whose work is done—spirit of dreadful hours!   80

The last sunbeam   64

The noble sire fallen on evil days   37

This dust was once the man   16

To the leaven'd soil they trod calling I sing for
  the last   83

Turn O Libertad, for the war is over   82

Vigil strange I kept on the field one night   49

When lilacs last in the dooryard bloom'd   3

While my wife at my side lies slumbering, and the
    wars are over long   69

Who are you, dusky woman, so ancient hardly
    human   71

With its cloud of skirmishers in advance   46

Word over all, beautiful as the sky   74

World take good notice, silver stars fading   73

Year that trembled and reel'd beneath me!   55